Where We Left Off

Jason Heroux & Michael Glover

Where We Left Off

– a mystically woven poetry collaboration between
Jason Heroux & Michael Glover

Copyright ©Jason Heroux & Michael Glover 2024
The moral rights of the authors have been asserted.
Cover image © Ruth Dupré
Caricatures and deformities after Leonardo. Two distorted heads, circa 1645, Flanders, by Wenceslaus Hollar, Leonardo da Vinci. Gift of Bishop Monrad, 1869. Te Papa (1869-0001-211)

www.1889books.co.uk
ISBN: 978-1-915045-38-6

Other publications by Jason Heroux

Memoirs of an Alias (2004)
Emergency Hallelujah (2008)
Good Evening, Central Laundromat (2010)
Natural Capital (2012)
Hard Work Cheering Up Sad Machines (2016)
Amusement Park of Constant Sorrow (2018)
Survivors of the Hive (2023)
Like a Trophy from the Sun (2024)

Other publications by Michael Glover

Poetry :

Measured Lives (1994)
Impossible Horizons (1995)
A Small Modicum of Folly (1997)
The Bead-Eyed Man (1999)
Amidst All This Debris (2001)
For the Sheer Hell of Living (2008)
Only So Much (2011)
Hypothetical May Morning (2018)
Messages to Federico (2018)
What You Do With Days (2019)
One Season in Hell (2020)
The Timely Lift-Off of the Famous Harlequin-Fish (2022)
Mistaking You for a Shower of Summer Confetti (2024)
Vincent's Poets (2024)

Others :

Headlong into Pennilessness (2011)
Great Works: Encounters with Art (2016)
Playing Out in the Wireless Days (2017)
111 Places in Sheffield You Shouldn't Miss (2017)
Late Days (2018)
Neo Rauch (2019)

The Book of Extremities (2019)
Thrust (2019)
John Ruskin: an idiosyncratic dictionary (2019)
Rose Wylie (2020)
Whose? (2020)
The Trapper (2021)
Nellie's Devils and Other Stories (2022)
794 Mini Sagas (2023)
The Skittery Zipper (2023)
111 Hidden Art Treasures of London (2024)

As editor or contributor :

Memories of Duveen Brothers (1976)
Goin' down, down, down: Matthew Ronay (2006)
Between Eagles and Pioneers: Georg Baselitz (2011)
Robert Therrien (2016)
Monique Frydman (2017)
A Garland of Poems for Christmas (2022)

Where We Left Off

For Jason

Is it unusual to begin like this?
I still like your photograph,
The way you are glancing away,
As if the noises off
Are what really matter once again.

Were we of a similar age, once?
I doubt that for a fact.
Whatever… It needn't stop
Us in our tracks,
This belief on my part, I meant to say,

That I may still be *The Ancient of Days*,
And you, perhaps,
With that characteristic
Lightness of heel step,
My distant brother's
Estranged younger son…

Would you like that?
'Like' in the way that an ice cream
Is welcome, mid-morning say,
Beneath a broiling sky
In the mid-day sun?

I would.
So let's drive off.
Wisconsin, did I hear you ask?
Well, why not?
You have all the dash these days – and some.
We can order more chipboard
If it ever comes to that…

Michael Glover

Where We Left Off

For Michael

*If something continues from where it left off,
it starts happening again at the point where
it had previously stopped.*
                    - Collins Dictionary

Where we left off is where we begin.
The lemon ends in its seed, the needle
returns to its thread. The falling rain

stops so that it can start to fall again.
The bell rings to make a sound,
the sound grows quiet until it's gone.

What's gone is still always going on.
Everything missing is found in the end.
The echoes rise from a canyon, hair

keeps growing on a barbershop floor.
Spiders never finish building their webs.
Everything found was missing before.

Our distant memories grow nearer
the further we get, departed friends
return in order to start to depart again.

Some other yesterday will visit us.
Some other sun will rise in the west.
What's done always has more to do.

Jason Heroux

Hooked Thumbs

You gave us your fistful
Of songs by moonlight,
More than enough,
Old-time crooners' numbers,
Until you turned hoarse and breathless.

It was then, when the cold came on,
That we wheeled you back in,
To the TV screen and the oxygen.
You would sleep then for hours on end,

And I would sit beside you, slumped,
Following the game shows lightly,
Thumb hooked into your thumb,
Old pals together again.

Michael Glover

Hooked Thumbs

I handed you an open hand
of quiet shadow,
less than sufficient,
a new-time tune that left you
calm and mellow.

A little later the heat turned on,
and we rolled you out
to a drive-in theatre underground.
You lay awake forever,

and I left you there, upright,
chased by the heavy starlight,
little finger freed from your finger,
new strangers separated for now.

Jason Heroux

Saying Goodbye to Frank O' Hara

I left off reading O'Hara when I left you.
It just didn't seem right to carry on.
I had my own throwaways to contend with.

After all, we are two men amongst men, aren't we,
With books, trophies, and brass tacks to prove it?

I ran a mile once,
Reaching the edge of the page
The day after yesterday,

Which brings me back, and up short,
To the nowness of here of course,
With this sentence still half cooked,

And too much steam about
To make my way around this kitchen
Without falling, face first, badly.

Poets, being clownish sorts,
Make too much of embarrassment.

Michael Glover

Saying Goodby to Frank O'Hara

I began reading O'Hara when we met.
It felt good to give up.
My forgotten harvest ready to yield.

Even then, we were two zeroes among none
with a lot of nothing to prove.

I sat a moment once,
in the heart of the matter
many years from now,

and never returned from where I still am.
Here where taking some leisurely stroll
alone through the mist is no alibi,

and the stunned silence of wonder
is no defence against what's next.

Bored poets, sad clowns, innocent
outlaws, suspects, accomplices, all of us
waiting for our sentences to be served.

Jason Heroux

Downhill to the Cataraqui River

It was those strolls through old Kingston, of course,
Which kept us together,
Down from Frontenac close to the lake –
Remember the toe-freeze of that straight-down,
Wall-clinging, cast-iron ladder into the water? –
And then on to Princess Street,
That gentle downhill slope
As far as the soothing name of the Cataraqui River....

It was generally sunny, being summer,
When we paused for coffee upstairs at Indigo's,
With the rummage sale of books
Spread out on a table –
A Pound, Ezra (some letters), I remember,
Not quite bought then, and forever regretted –
All those spine-up enticements,
Quite close to the window...

And then on to my first jaccuzi –
The steam, bounce and frisk of hot hot water! –
At the Holiday Inn,
Followed by a little potted history
In the company of Macdonald's spirit
At City Hall, and then to drinks on a terrace lake-facing,
Three too many, before retiring to
The shady courtyard of Chez Piggy
For a thick-as-thieves hunkering down
Over bowls of clam chowder...

We talked of book titles, our favourites,
And both agreed it just had to be Charles Simic:
Return to a Place Lit by a Glass of Milk.
The Serbo-Yankee poet had nailed it!
If that milk hadn't been so guileless,
We might well have drunk it,
And stolen the title too
If it hadn't been chosen already.

Michael Glover

Downhill to the Cataraqui River

At this time due to the increased demand for poetry, some poems are taking longer than normal to write. Although there may not be any guaranteed timeline in regards to when this particular poem way appear, please be assured that its composition remains a high priority, and is currently in process. Kindly revisit this page as needed for frequent status updates and further information. In the meantime may we suggest reading one of the many other poems in this book. The piece on the previous page, for example, also happens to be titled "Downhill to the Cataraqui River" and is readily available to be read again. Thank you for your support, patience, and understanding. Sincerely, Management.

Jason Heroux

Big Jim

When Big Jim, slick in retail,
Steered us both down the highway
With his knees as far as the ball game in Toronto,
He knocked the Red Sox clean out of the park

Before tonning us back home at speed,
while still singing *I'm as much a man as ever, Darlin'*…
Truth is, I have never not admired him.

Michael Glover

Big Jim

When I met Big Jim he took
one look at my shadow, faded and worn
around the edges, and said
I can get you a great deal on a new one.

He led me to the rack, helped
pick out a new shade that fit perfectly.
It was so well made, I still wear it today.
Truth is, it will likely last longer than me.

Jason Heroux

Interlude

You asked again, through a gap in the clouds.
What was I to do? Stop running?

It all comes on so suddenly,
And most of it made of paper
Too fragile to be waved in any wind.

You recognise a burial these days by the humming.

Michael Glover

Interlude

I stand on my shore, and witness no other.
Here where the river's echo flows

to the sea of its voice, and the falling leaf
lives endlessly in the leaf, falling on and on.

The water breaks, recovers, shatters, heals.
A rain puddle lies nearby, an infant

lake, hungry and awake in its crib of grass.
A distant windmill grinds the sky to ground.

I stand on no shore, and witness
another, where the wind is always passing,

but never past, and now has nowhere to be.
Where the smoke has risen, a fire once was.

Every road endures beyond dirt and gravel.
What's left is still around, but it's not ours.

Return my happiness to where it's from,
give my ring to the bell that made its sound.

Jason Heroux

Singing All Day

To drive is to see as far as you need to go.
There is no end to it – until the steering wheel
Comes clean off in your hands,
And the roadside shack winks its fond lamp at you,
Whereupon you duly enter, doff your cap (peaked),
And gladly accept a glass or two.

There are old stories, many, to be listened to,
And the crushed racoon to be buried,
The latest in a long string of local accidents.
Meanwhile, the spillway has run dry,
The oldsters tell you,
Which is why now there is only ever the local rye
To be drunk, so you have to settle for that
And/or sing, all the live-long day,
Of the love there has always been
Between just the two of you.

Michael Glover

Singing All Day

{Verse}
G
I stared ahead at yesterday's snow
                                    Em
Melting in the sun, blazing bright,
      C   G
With a dying fire from the past.
                    D
How it burned, but remained.
      G
A fire without fuel, or smoke,
       Em
Or heat, or ash, a flame of no.

{Chorus}
C   G
It hurt to gaze, so I looked away.
      D   G
The way a leaf looks away
G
From the wind, or a star
          Em
Looks away from the dark.

{Repeat Verse}

{Repeat Chorus}

{All Day}

Jason Heroux

Old Rocking

I've a mind to tell you a story this morning,
Old rocker, by which I mean
Of the wooden, front-porch variety,
Which is where I happen to be sitting,
The van having just driven away
Heaped high with all the things
Belonging to my son's half-brother,
Yes, I took him in, and now he's gone,
And thereby hangs a tale
Set fair for a day other than this one,
Since you're asking…

What shall we speak of then?
Of the here and now?
There's precious little of it
That tastes sweet these days,
Too much of an ill wind
That never stops blowing,
Too much of the sameyness of stale bread –
All those over-long pauses between the pauses.
You get my meaning.
I wouldn't be telling you of all this
If I didn't know you were listening.

You just told me you were still listening.

Michael Glover

Old Rocking

What's your story, old rocker?
I want to know.
Tell me what you're thinking
perched on the front porch,
under the sun, or the clouds,
or the stars, depending
on the time and weather
of the world.

Tell me what
makes you totter and sway
with such gentle momentum.

Your body, at rest, remained
at rest, until I sat together with you
at the end of another weary day.
We applied a force to each other
for hours, old friend, a rhythm
of equal magnitude
and opposite direction.

Tell me why we creak and grow
loose with time under all
the pressure that brings us back
to life.

Jason Heroux

Meaning Things

I wouldn't have said it
If I hadn't meant it.
Old men like me,
We mean things by our words.
Nothing comes lightly
When you have the dead weight
Of a lifetime to contend with.

So come and see what I've made of it,
The vegetable patch in the back garden,
See how much is flourishing –
Green shoots of spring,
Hardy and keen as spears
To kill a thousand ancient Macedonians!
If you had an appetite for such things.
I am inclined to walk away from conflict.
Get an eyeful of this, youngsters:
Killing cures nothing.

Michael Glover

Meaning Things

I wouldn't have said octopus
if I hadn't meant orangutang.
Old dolphins like us,
we sing things to our songs.
Everything goes darkly
when you have the living light
of sleep to dream about.

So go make what has come of you,
little garden sewn into the dirt.
See how little you've withered -
black spade of spring,
your flat blade open
as an ear digging into the compact
sound of an earthworm's ancient song!
If you had a bucket for such water.
I'd rather raise myself up from the well.
Open your eyes, ghosts:
living cures everything.

Jason Heroux

Every New Day

Every day I do try
To be a little more truthful.
What is the point of lying?
I first saw you out there
In the garden in April.
Two years on, add on
An extra month or two,
We were married.
You could fact-check that
If you felt so inclined.

I loved you for a lifetime,
And I am still loving you.
I see you where you are not.
I raise a glass to you.
I even raise a broken cup,
Your broken cup.
You are never not here with me.
You could fact-check all that
If you felt so inclined.

Yesterday the weather was maungy.
I sat inside with a flickering screen
And a new book, barely touched…
There's a gap in the door
Where the wind blows through.
I tried to fix it.
Is this a diary I am writing?
Or is it a conversation,
Barely begun before finished?
I'm asking you.
Feel free to ask back.
And fact-check too
If you're not sure
It's me still speaking.

Michael Glover

Every New Day

The snow-covered sidewalk
wakes and smokes
a pack of footprints,

city buses are drawn
like moths to a bus stop's flame.
Every new day finds us.

The wind's freshly pressed
dress-shirt puts on its body.
The way an infant turtle hatched

in sand finds its path to the sea,
every buttonhole embraces
its button, every cup of tea

recites its silent
prayer of steam.

Jason Heroux

Incident at the Roadside

Just down there,
A little up the road I mean,
There's a young man standing talking.
He's waiting for something.
He's muttering into his sleeve.
No, he's talking to Jesus.
No, he's barking into his phone
With overmuch passion!
I see him slice down with his thumb
As if he's cutting someone.

Then he drops it and looks down,
And then looks up again.
A car has drawn up
With all the quiet smoothness of patience.
A woman gets out, twice his age and some.
She levers him into a seat at the back, saying:
Calmness, calmness, darling…
At least, that's what I think she is saying.

Michael Glover

Incident at the Roadside

After all these many years
the incident at the roadside
has no incident, and is simply
a roadside.

The ditch grass sways in wind.
Crickets hop across the gravel.
No one is talking to Jesus.
No one is standing around
muttering into their sleeve.

The incident is now nowhere
to be found, no trace, forgotten
as if it never happened.

Roadside, remind us
we are where earthworms thirst
for dirt, far from home.

As if the car never drew up.
As if the woman never got out,
and said, *Calmness, calmness, darling…*

Remind us the roadside is our world.

Jason Heroux

The Red House, Over Yonder…

Don't do it, not just yet, Jason…
Don't leave until you've turned out your last pocket.
I'm facing you over a beer-slicked table top
In Kingston, in The Red House as they call it,
Which means that Jimi's playing,
Except that he's not,
Which is part of the problem.

If Jimi were here with us now,
Pouring his gorgeous blues notes into our ears,
We'd be smiling,
And all would be smoothly paradisal.
As it is, this silence means
That we don't have two cents left between us,
Not any more,
Not with all these dead beer bottles
Rolling around us.

Michael Glover

The Red House, Over Yonder …

There must be
some kind of way out.

The key won't unlock
this door.
Lately things don't seem
the same.

I have only one burning desire.
But I don't know how to go about getting it,

with a circus mind that's running wild.

Is that the stars in the sky, or is it
rain falling down? Fall mountains,
just don't fall on me.

The tiny island sags downstream.

Make everything back together,
strange beautiful grass of green

Jason Heroux

Thursday Evening

Because I want it all to be happening here again,
Now that it's so much quieter
Than it always used to be.
I want us to be cycling into the wind –
Or is the wind at our backs,
Urging us on? Yes, probably that.

And then I want you to be speeding up,
Coming parallel with me!
We're both racing the wind,
on and on and on…
And then what happens next?
Years just slip away
Without anyone even noticing.

The mortgage gets paid off.
The children visit, intermittently.
We crack open a bottle of wine
Once a week, on a Thursday evening,
Six o'clock, sharpish.
And this, believe it or not,
Is that Thursday evening.

Michael Glover

Thursday Evening

Thursday evening, hold tight.
A change is coming your way.
Do you remember
what happened to Wednesday?
It was here, laughing, not a care
in the world. And now it's gone.

The same will happen to you,
and me, and all of us. Look
at your sky, it's already starting
to darken. Listen to your traffic
growing quieter and quieter.
Your clouds are the grey ghosts
of clouds still to come.

But you still have time,
it's only six o'clock, someone
has opened a bottle of wine,
and believe it or not, there are poems
being written about you, and many dear
friends are gathered around to hear them.

Jason Heroux